WAY

Henry Hudson

Henry Hudson

Andrew Santella

Watts LIBRARY

Franklin Watts
A Division of Scholastic Inc.
New York • Toronto • London • Auckland • Sydney
Mexico City • New Delhi • Hong Kong
Danbury, Connecticut

Note to readers: Definitions for words in **bold** can be found in the Glossary at the back of this book.

Photographs ©: Corbis-Bettmann: 16 (Galen Powell), 28, 34, 35; Crown Copyright/National Monuments Record: 6; Mary Evans Picture Library: 5 bottom, 51 (Edwin Wallace Collection), 22, 39, 44, 53; North Wind Picture Archives: 5 top, 8, 9, 11, 18, 30, 33, 36, 38, 41; Photo Researchers, NY/Tom McHugh: 20; Stock Montage, Inc.: 2, 12, 24, 42, 43; Visuals Unlimited: 49 (Tim Hauf Photography), 26 (Fritz Polking), 27 (Rob & Ann Simpson), 50 (L. S. Stepanowicz), 37 (Ned Therrien), 14, 15.

Cover illustration by Stephen Marchesi.

Map by XNR Productions, Inc.

The illustration on the cover shows Henry Hudson in North America. The illustration opposite the title page shows a portrait of Henry Hudson.

Library of Congress Cataloging-in-Publication Data

Santella, Andrew.
    Henry Hudson / Andrew Santella.
        p. cm. — (Watts Library)
    Includes bibliographical references and index.
    ISBN 0-531-11968-8 (lib. bdg.)   0-531-16577-9 (pbk.)
    1. Hudson, Henry, d. 1611—Juvenile literature. 2. America—Discovery and exploration—English—Juvenile literature. 3. Explorers—America—Biography—Juvenile literature. 4. Explorers—England—Biography—Juvenile literature. [1. Hudson, Henry, d. 1611. 2. Explorers. 3. America—Discovery and Exploration—English.] I. Title. II. Series.
E129.H8 S26 2001
910'.92—dc21

                                         [B]
                                   00-043781

Contents

St. Ethelburga's church has stood in London since the 1300s.

Chapter One

A Passage to Asia

On April 19, 1607, twelve sailors gathered in St. Ethelburga's Church in London, England. They were about to go to sea. Ships' crews of those days often went to church together before going on long or difficult trips. These sailors were about to make one of the most dangerous journeys of their lives.

Their ship was called the *Hopewell*, and their captain was named Henry Hudson. As Hudson and his crew prayed in church that morning, they probably tried not to think about the hardships that waited for them on the open sea. They would sail into crippling cold temperatures. Huge icebergs might destroy their wooden ship. Even the best maps of their day would be of little help in the vast unknown waters they intended to sail.

Hudson and his crew planned on sailing from England to Asia by way of the North Pole. No one in history had made this journey. No one knew if it was possible—but Hudson was determined to find out if it could be done.

Searching for a Route to Asia

Like many explorers of his time, Hudson wanted to find a passage through the northern seas to Asia. This goal became his life's work. Four times, he sailed through icy oceans looking for such a passage. He sailed farther north than anyone ever had before. He explored new places, including a river and a bay in North America that now bear his name. But he never found a northern passage to Asia.

Hudson lived in a time of great explorations by Europeans. Europeans of the 1500s and 1600s ventured far into unknown lands

It was dangerous for ships to sail the icy northern seas.

and uncharted waters. They were curious about the world beyond the horizon. They were also eager to profit from their discoveries. For centuries, Europeans had benefited from trade with Asia. Silk made its way overland from China to Europe. Many of the precious metals that Europeans used for money came from Asia. Most of all, Europeans wanted spices from eastern Asia.

Long before refrigeration, food tended to smell bad and taste worse. Europeans learned that spices such as **cloves, cinnamon,** and **cardamom** made food edible. Many of those spices came from the Moluccas Islands. The Moluccas are located about halfway between the Philippines and Australia. Europeans found so many spices in the Moluccas that they called them the Spice Islands.

International trade was a tricky business. Trade routes could be shut down and trade disrupted. That's exactly what happened in 1453, with the Ottoman capture of the city of Constantinople. Because of its location, many trade routes to and from Asia went through Constantinople. When the Ottomans took control of Constantinople, they also took control of Europe's trade. That meant Europeans could no longer get the **goods** they desired from the East. They had to find another route to Asia.

Spain and Portugal controlled the southern sea routes to Asia. England and other European countries turned to the northern seas to find their own route to Asia. Their search was costly. Several explorers lost their lives in the frigid North. An

Constantinople

Constantinople was located on the Bosporus, a **strait** that many people considered the dividing line between Asia and Europe. Today the city is called Istanbul, and it is the largest city in Turkey.

The Dangerous North

Dutch explorer Willem Barents sailed along the northern coast of Russia three times to find a way to Asia. On his third trip, his ship became trapped in huge ice **floes**. This illustration shows his crew trying to navigate the icy waters.

Barents and his crew spent the winter of 1596–1597 in crude cabins they built on the frozen shore of Novaya Zemlya. The cabins offered little protection from the harsh climate. Barents died—a victim of the cold.

Englishman named John Davis had better luck. He sailed between Greenland and Canada on three voyages in the 1580s, looking for a passage to Asia. He didn't find the passage, but he did make important discoveries that would help the sailors who would follow. Some historians believe that Henry Hudson was among his crew on one of those trips.

Hudson's Early Years

The English merchants in this illustration are looking at a map. Can you guess why they sponsored voyages of exploration?

Not much is known about Hudson's early life. Not even his date of birth is recorded. He was probably born in the 1570s, possibly in Hoddersdon, about 17 miles (27 kilometers) northwest of London. English **merchants** sponsored voyages of exploration when Hudson was a young man. Historians believe his family was part of a group of merchants that sent several ships in search of a northern passage to Asia. The

group was named the Merchant Adventurers. His grandfather was probably one of its founders.

A man named Thomas Hudson, who may have been related to Henry Hudson, was captain of a ship owned by the Merchant Adventurers. As a boy, Henry may have served on such a ship. If so, he would have learned firsthand how dangerous the northern seas could be. On these early trips, he may have become determined to find a northern passage to Asia.

None of the Merchant Adventurers found such a passage. The group did secure trading rights with Russia, however. Soon the group became known as the Muscovy Company. The group was named for Moscow, a Russian city.

In 1607, the Muscovy Company sponsored Hudson's first voyage as a captain. This voyage would be his chance to pursue the greatest prize of all for an English **mariner**—the discovery of a passage to Asia through the icy waters of the North.

Henry Hudson wanted to sail to Asia by way of the North Pole.

Chapter Two

Toward the North Pole

Hudson's instructions from the Muscovy Company were clear. He was "to discover a passage by the North Pole to Japan and China." Today, we know the North Pole is a region of forbidding cold and ice, but explorers did not reach the North Pole until centuries after Hudson sailed. In Hudson's time, some explorers and mapmakers believed that cutting across the North Pole would be the easiest way to reach Asia. They based their ideas on the fact that the summer sun

Holes in the Ice

Peter Plancius and Robert Thorne were wrong about **navigable** waters near the North Pole, but holes do form in the ice at the North Pole. In 2000, visitors to the North Pole saw a 1-mile (2-km) wide lake in the ice. The melting heat of the sun and the force of wind and waves create cracks in the ice. Sometimes those cracks widen to become larger holes, as this photograph shows.

shines on the North Pole for twenty-four hours each day. Under that constant sunshine, they reasoned, the North Pole could not possibly be covered by ice. A geographer named Robert Thorne even made a map showing how ships could sail a warm-water, navigable sea near the North Pole.

A Dutch geographer named Peter Plancius agreed. He wrote that "near the Pole the sun shines five months continually and although his rays are weak . . . they have sufficient strength to warm the ground." Plancius and Thorne thought that if a ship could just get through the ice and fog of the North Atlantic, it would find smoother sailing closer to the North Pole. Then it would be a short trip to the Pacific Ocean and Asia. This was the route that the Muscovy Company sent Henry Hudson to find in 1607.

Hudson and his crew would make the trip to the North Pole in a type of ship called a **bark**. The *Hopewell* was a small, wooden ship with three masts. The ship was three years old, and it had sailed six other voyages.

On Board the *Hopewell*

Life on board the *Hopewell* was difficult. The sailors slept in cramped quarters. They lived on supplies of food that could spoil quickly.

Because the crew could not drink saltwater from the ocean, they had to depend on supplies of freshwater stored in **casks**. After a few weeks at sea, the water might be covered by a film of scum. The English explorer Sir Walter Raleigh wrote that sailors must endure "a hard cabin, cold and salt meat (often crawling with maggots), mouldy biscuit.... wet clothes and want of fire for cooking and warmth."

Henry Hudson sailed the east coast of Greenland and described it as a "very high land for the most part covered in snow, the remaining part bare."

Into the Unknown

Hudson set sail from London on May 1, 1607. He directed the *Hopewell* northwest toward Greenland. The east coast of Greenland had not been explored yet, and Hudson wanted to map it. He was not sailing in ideal conditions for exploration, however. The fog was so thick that Hudson could not see where his ship was going. Still, he sailed on blindly. The wind picked up and brought new trouble. In the choppy seas, the sails became wet. Then they froze. So did the ropes and **rigging** the crew had to use to sail the ship. Coated with jagged ice, they cut into the crew's hands. The ship's journal records the horrible weather Hudson's crew had to endure every day. June 13: "It rained all that afternoon and evening." June 14: "Today we had much wind and rain." June 15: "Very much rain."

When the weather cleared, Hudson sailed away from Greenland. He headed northeast toward Spitsbergen. Spitsbergen is a group of islands well north of the Arctic Circle. Spitsbergen was so remote that Dutch sailors had just discovered it eleven years earlier. As Hudson neared the islands, he found his way blocked by floating ice. The *Hopewell*

Spitsbergen

Dutch whalers discovered Spitsbergen in 1596. Now called Svalbard, Spitsbergen is part of Norway. There are four main islands and about 150 smaller ones located about 400 miles (640 km) north of Norway. Glaciers cover about sixty percent of this region.

Hudson probably saw beluga whales because they inhabit the Arctic Ocean and its adjoining seas.

finally reached Spitsbergen by the end of June 1607. There to greet the ship were more whales than Hudson had ever seen. He noted the whales in his journals. After his report reached England, English ships were soon harvesting the whales of Spitsbergen for oil. Barely ten years later, there were few whales left near Spitsbergen.

Turning Back

By the middle of July 1607, Hudson reached the northern tip of Spitsbergen. They were now just 577 miles (929 km) from the North Pole. No one had ever sailed that far north, but Hudson could go no farther. He found his way north blocked by ice. On July 16, he wrote in his journal, "there is no passage by this way." Eleven days later, the *Hopewell* narrowly avoided a collision with a huge iceberg. Hudson decided to head back to England. By mid-September, the *Hopewell* was back home.

The crew of the *Hopewell* had been at sea for more than four months. Hudson had sailed farther north than anyone before. He had seen enough to convince him that there was no passage to Asia by way of the North Pole, but he was not finished looking for other water routes to the East.

Among the Whales

At times, the *Hopewell* sailed among so many whales that the animals actually jostled the ship. Hudson wrote, "We saw many whales in this bay, and while one of the crew had a hook and line overboard to try and catch fish, a whale came up under the keel of the ship and got caught . . . by God's mercy we were unharmed."

Each crew member aboard a ship had different responsibilities. Among the sailors on Hudson's 1608 journey were a boatswain, carpenter, and cook.

Chapter Three

The Northeast Passage

Henry Hudson's first attempt at a passage to Asia had failed, but in the spring of 1608, he was ready to try again. This time, he would head northeast, along the northern coast of Russia. Once more, he would sail the *Hopewell*, and the Muscovy Company would sponsor the trip.

Hudson had the *Hopewell* strengthened with extra planks to better withstand icy waters. He hired a new, larger crew. This time, fifteen people would sail on the *Hopewell*. Only three of them had

Mermaids

Mermaids were an important part of sailors' legends. They were supposed to be female sea creatures with the upper body of a woman and the tail of a fish. Some sailors believed that mermaids could create storms, floods, and other deadly weather. Others believed that mermaids sang so beautifully that they could lure sailors into the sea, where they would drown.

sailed with Hudson on his first trip. The new crew left London on April 22, 1608, and they soon encountered hardship. The *Hopewell* had been at sea just a few weeks when floating ice began to make sailing difficult. The crew struggled in the damp and cold, but sickness forced four of them to stay in their bunks. In early June, the *Hopewell* was almost surrounded and crushed by floating ice.

The sailors saw more than ice at sea. Two of Hudson's crew sighted a mermaid. Hudson described the creature as if there was no doubt that mermaids existed. "Her [upper body was] like a woman's," he wrote. "Her body as big as ours, her skin very white, and she had long black hair hanging down behind. When she dove they saw her tail which was like the tail of a porpoise, and speckled like a mackerel." Hudson said that the mermaid was "calling the rest of the crew to come see her."

Sailing through Ice

Mermaids were the least of the crew's concerns. As the *Hopewell* headed northeast, the crew spent entire days weaving in and out of ice fields. They needed their best sailing skills to navigate the treacherous northern seas. One wrong move and ice could pierce the ship's **hull**, and the crew would be lost. The ice grew even thicker as they neared the islands of Novaya Zemlya, off the coast of Russia. Hudson intended to sail around Novaya Zemlya. On the other side of the islands, he believed he would find a sea that would lead him to the Pacific Ocean. The heavy ice prevented Hudson from sailing

Novaya Zemlya

Novaya Zemlya means "new land" in Russian.

25

Hunters kill walruses for their flesh, oil, skin, intestines, tusks, and bones.

Walrus Hunt

Because they live in groups of up to one hundred, walruses are easy marks for hunters.

north, so he began looking for another way around the islands. As he sailed, he spotted walruses lounging on the floating ice. Hudson had some of his crew try to hunt the walruses, but they were only able to kill one. However, more hunters would follow Hudson's route. In a few years, the walruses of Novaya Zemlya suffered the same fate as the whales of Spitsbergen.

On July 2, 1608, Hudson thought he saw a way to get to the sea on the other side of the largest island. He would go not around the island, but through it. He spotted a "fair river" running through the island "six to nine miles broad." He turned the *Hopewell* into the river to explore. The ship hadn't gone far when great chunks of ice began to float toward it. Pushed by a strong current, the ice would crush the *Hopewell*

Icebergs come in all shapes and sizes—irregular, rounded, and tabular.

if it made contact with her. Hudson's crew desperately tried to keep the ice away from the ship. They pushed the ice away with oars and beams and finally worked the ship to safety.

As it turned out, the river did not cut through the island— it led only to a landlocked bay, filled with yet more ice. Hudson's journal entry conveys his disappointment: "My hope was that the strength of current would have kept [the water] cleared of ice, but it did not. It is so full of ice you would hardly believe it. All day it was foggy and cold."

Heading West

Hudson gave up on finding a passage along the coast of Russia. He turned the *Hopewell* around, but he did not head straight for England. Instead, he sailed west into the Atlantic Ocean toward North America. He had led his crew through two months of hard sailing through icy waters, but he wasn't ready to give up. He still wanted to look for a passage to Asia

This illustration shows a mutiny—sailors refusing to obey their captain.

in the waters north of North America. The weather was not in Hudson's favor. Day after day, the *Hopewell* sailed through rain and rough seas. Soon his crew turned against him. When they realized they weren't returning to England, they grew angry. Hudson was determined to keep going, but he couldn't do it alone. He needed his crew to obey his orders. Some historians believe that Hudson's crew refused to obey his orders. They left him no choice but to return home.

Disobeying a captain's orders is one of the worst offenses a sailor can commit. If the authorities found out the sailors of the *Hopewell* had mutinied against Hudson, the sailors could be hanged. Hudson presented his crew with a document that stated he had turned the *Hopewell* around without any "persuasion or force by any one or more of them." The crew may have demanded that Hudson write the note so they would be protected against charges of mutiny. By the end of August 1608, Hudson and crew were back in England. Not surprisingly, Henry Hudson was deeply disappointed—but he wasn't ready to give up.

Mutiny

Sailors defying a captain's authority could be executed without a trial.

Manhattan, now part of New York City, looked quite different in Hudson's day.

chapter Four

The River of Mountains

On his first two voyages, Hudson had sailed mainly along deserted coastlines in the frozen north. His third voyage would take him into the interior of North America. There he would explore the river that now bears his name. He would also sail past the site of what would one day be New York City.

Hudson was miserable after the failure of his first two voyages. A friend wrote that Hudson had "sunk into the lowest depths . . . from which no man could rouse him . . . I told him he had created Fame that would endure for all time, but he would not listen to me."

Hudson wasn't the only one disappointed with his failure. His sponsors at the Muscovy Company had had enough of unsuccessful exploratory voyages. Hudson would have to find someone else to support his search for a passage to Asia. He set his sights on the Dutch East India Company.

The Dutch East India Company

Like the Muscovy Company, the Dutch East India Company traded goods with other countries. The Dutch East India Company was larger, richer, and more powerful than the Muscovy Company. The Dutch East India Company owned a fleet of forty large ships and many more small ones, and it employed 5,000 sailors. The Dutch East India's **charter** with the government of Holland even gave the company the right to wage war. The Dutch company's ships were already actively trading with Asia, and its ships had made the long journey around the Cape of Good Hope at the southern tip of Africa. However, the Dutch East India Company was looking for a shorter route.

Sailing Under Other Flags

Henry Hudson was not the only sea captain to sail for a country other than his own. Christopher Columbus was an Italian sailing for Spain. Sebastian Cabot was an Italian sailing for England and Spain. Giovanni da Verrazano was an Italian in French service.

On January 8, 1609, the Dutch East India Company agreed to pay Hudson to search for a passage to Asia with one condition. Hudson's contract stated that he was "to think of discovering no other route or passage, except the route around the north or northeast above Novaya Zembla." Hudson was to look for the passage along the northern coast of Russia, from where he had just returned.

Hudson's new Dutch employers probably knew about his eagerness to explore North America. They wanted him to

The Dutch East India Company formed in 1602 and soon became a powerful force in European trade.

This engraving shows Henry Hudson receiving his contract from the Dutch East India Company.

stick to the plan they had agreed upon—exploring the northern coast of Russia. Hudson signed the contract, but it would take more than a contract to keep Hudson from heading west toward North America.

The *Half Moon*

The Dutch East India Company gave Hudson a small, aging ship called the *Half Moon*. One director of the company complained that "she will prove difficult to handle in foul weather." Hudson complained too, but he was stuck with the *Half Moon*. He would also have to make do with a crew that was split between English and Dutch sailors. Hudson did not even speak Dutch. The *Half Moon* set sail from Amsterdam on April 6, 1609, and conflicts soon erupted between the English and Dutch crew members. Cold weather and rough seas blocked the ship's route. The Dutch crew was used to the calmer waters of the southern seas, and they grumbled about the rough conditions. Some

This illustration shows the Half Moon *sailing from Amsterdam in 1609.*

wanted to turn around and head home.

Some captains would have considered such complaints mutiny. Hudson saw his crew's complaints as an opportunity to change the goal of the trip. He assembled his crew and showed them maps of North America. He explained that this was where he really wanted to go. The crew agreed, figuring that at least it would be warmer there. So Hudson ignored his contract, turned the *Half Moon* around, and headed for North America.

North America

By July 1609, the ship was off the coast of Canada. On July 18, Hudson's crew went ashore at Penobscot Bay in what is now Maine. They spent a week there, making repairs to the *Half Moon*'s **mast** and catching lobsters. They also met some Penobscot Indians.

Hudson headed toward Virginia, where he believed he would find a strait that led to the Pacific Ocean. Through late July and into August, Hudson sailed up and down the East

Hudson and the Penobscots

Hudson's crew was suspicious of the Penobscot Indians they met. "We could not trust them," one of the sailors wrote. Before Hudson's crew left the coast of Maine, they drove the Penobscots from their homes and robbed them. Then the crew sailed south. The Penobscots were left behind, empty-handed and betrayed.

Coast, looking for the strait. On September 3, 1609, he spotted a wide river. Later, he called it the "River of Mountains." Local Indians called it Muhheakunnuk, which means "great waters constantly in motion." Today we call it the Hudson River. Hudson was at the site of present-day New York City. He claimed the area for the Dutch, then took a look around.

This photograph shows Penobscot Bay near Camden, Maine.

Lenape Indians greeted Hudson and his crew when they went ashore at the Hudson River.

Up the Hudson River

Hudson met some Lenape Indians, and they gave him his first taste of American corn. Hudson's crew traded beads and knives for Indian tobacco. The next day, Hudson sent five crew members in a small boat to explore another river. They were attacked by two canoes full of Lenape warriors. Hudson's crew rowed hard for the safety of the *Half Moon*. Before they could reach the ship, one of the sailors was shot through the throat with an arrow. Two others were seriously wounded. Hudson's crew finally drove the Indians away. They buried the dead sailor, John Coleman, the next day. Hudson decided to head upriver.

A week later, he was in view of the Catskill Mountains. There he went ashore and met with a Mahican chief. Hudson wrote, "Two mats were spread out to sit upon, and immediately some food was served in well-made red wooden bowls . . . They likewise killed a fat dog, and skinned it in great haste with shells which they had got out of the water." The Mahicans thought Hudson would stay with them for the night. When he got up to return to the ship, they assumed he was worried about being

Hudson accepts the Mahican chief's invitation for dinner.

Mahicans and Lenape

The Lenape lived along the Atlantic coast of what is now New Jersey. They had come in contact with Europeans long before Hudson's arrival. They met the explorer Giovanni da Verrazano when he explored the area in 1524. They had decades of bad experiences with some Europeans who raided the Lenape and other peoples for slaves. By the time Hudson arrived, they distrusted Europeans. So it was not long before they came into conflict with Hudson's crew. The Mahicans lived inland from the Atlantic Ocean. They had not had contact with Europeans before Hudson's arrival, so they weren't as hostile as the Lenape. Hudson was able to establish friendly relations with the Mahicans.

killed. To show him they meant no harm, they broke their arrows in half and tossed them onto the fire. Hudson wrote that the Mahicans were "a very good people."

As Hudson headed north, the river grew shallower. He soon realized that this river would not lead him to the Pacific Ocean. He would have to look elsewhere for his passage to Asia. Near the site of present-day Albany, New York, he turned the *Half Moon* around. As Hudson headed back to the Atlantic Ocean, he had one more conflict with American Indians. As the *Half Moon* neared the ocean, some coastal Indians boarded the ship to trade. One Indian stole some clothes from the ship's cabin. A crew member caught the thief and shot him. Hudson ordered the crew to sail a few miles away before stopping for the night. The next day, about one hundred Indians attacked the ship. The sailors drove them away with cannon and musket fire. One of the crew remem-

bered, "I shot a light cannon and killed two. The rest fled into the woods. They sent off another canoe manned by nine or ten. I sent off another shot from the cannon and killed one of them. Then our men with their muskets killed three or four more. They went their way. . . ."

On October 4, 1609, the *Half Moon* sailed out of the Hudson River and into the open sea. The *Half Moon*'s three

This illustration shows Hudson's crew firing upon American Indians near present-day Peekskill, New York.

months in North America had been very bloody. Winter was approaching, and Hudson decided it was time to return to Europe. As Hudson crossed the Atlantic Ocean, he must have been concerned about how his Dutch employers would receive him. After all, he had disobeyed their orders by sailing to North America. That may be why Hudson did not go straight to Holland. On November 7, 1609, he landed the *Half Moon* in Dartmouth, England. As it turned out, the English authorities held him in custody for sailing under the Dutch flag. They forbade Hudson from ever working for a foreign company, and they told him not to leave England. Hudson's third voyage had ended badly, but he would have one more chance.

This illustration shows the Half Moon *sailing on the Hudson River.*

Although the British East India Company sent Hudson to North America, the company was most influential in India.

Chapter Five

The Bay of Ice

A few months after his return to England, Hudson was ready to sail again. This time, he would have to find English backers and sail under the flag of England. He convinced some of the richest people in England to help pay for his next voyage. Five English noblemen supported the trip, including Prince Henry. The British East India Company provided a ship called the *Discovery* and had her overhauled in preparation for the trip. The *Discovery* was the largest ship Hudson had commanded. To sail her, Hudson employed twenty-two crew members, including his son John.

The Final Voyage

The goal of Hudson's fourth voyage was to look for a route to Asia in the waters of North America. On April 17, 1610, Prince Henry climbed aboard the *Discovery* to wish Hudson well. It was the last he or anyone in England would see of the explorer. Almost from the start, the voyage went badly. Rough weather stalled Hudson near Iceland. Then trouble erupted among the crew. Two sailors got into a fistfight, and Hudson took one's side against the other. Unhappy about this, a sailor named Robert Juet began defying Hudson's orders. The *Discovery* had been at sea for only a month, and events were spinning out of control.

Still, Hudson sailed on. By the end of June 1610, the *Discovery* had reached a body of water called the Furious Overfall. (Today it is called Hudson's Strait.) The Furious Overfall had been discovered by the explorer John Davis in 1587. He named it for the rushing torrents of water he had found there—conditions that made sailing there very risky for most of the year. Now Hudson had to deal with the same perils. A sailor named Abacuk Prickett wrote, "The tides and

Lewis and Clark

Two hundred years after Hudson sailed, two American explorers—Meriwether Lewis and William Clark—looked for a water route across North America in a **keel-boat** that they named *Discovery*. In 1804, Lewis and Clark traveled part of the way up the Missouri River in this vessel. They found no such route.

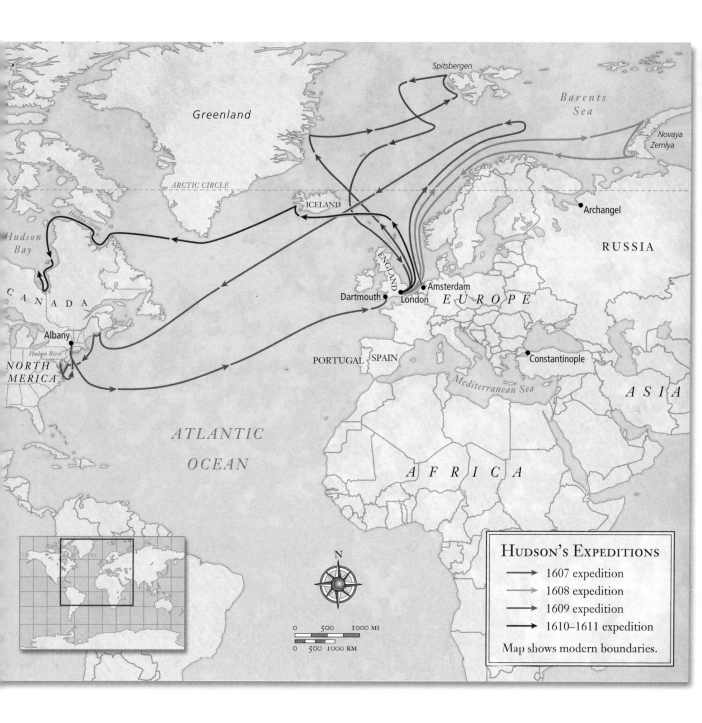

Greenland

Spitsbergen

Barents Sea

Novaya Zemlya

ARCTIC CIRCLE

ICELAND

• Archangel

RUSSIA

Hudson Strait

Hudson Bay

C A N A D A

ENGLAND

• Amsterdam
Dartmouth • London

E U R O P E

A S I A

Albany •

Hudson River

NORTH AMERICA

PORTUGAL   SPAIN

• Constantinople

Mediterranean Sea

ATLANTIC

OCEAN

A F R I C A

N

HUDSON'S EXPEDITIONS

→ 1607 expedition
→ 1608 expedition
→ 1609 expedition
→ 1610–1611 expedition

Map shows modern boundaries.

0   500   1000 MI
0   500 1000 KM

currents opened the ice, carrying it first one way then another." Storms rocked the ship. Thick fog made it impossible even to navigate. Several of his crew fell sick. Desperate, Hudson had the *Discovery* take shelter in a bay.

Then more trouble broke out. Trapped by ice, the crew of the *Discovery* began talking of returning home. Hudson had to do something, so he pulled out his maps and charts. He told his crew that they had traveled hundreds of miles farther than any other Englishmen. Then he told them he would let them decide if they should continue. Reluctantly, they agreed to travel on. By letting them decide for themselves, Hudson surrendered some of his authority.

Winter in a Strange Land

On August 2, 1610, the *Discovery* entered a strait between cliffs thousands of feet high. Then the strait widened and the ship "suddenly came into a great and whirling sea." Today we call it Hudson Bay. For a time, Hudson believed he had found the passage to Asia he had been looking for. For three months, the *Discovery* crept along the eastern coast of Hudson Bay. Hudson looked for some sign he was on the right track, but his hope slowly faded. By the end of October, the *Discovery* was trapped by ice at the southern tip of the bay.

Winter was approaching, and Hudson's crew was openly grumbling about their situation. He ordered two crew members to go ashore and find a place to wait out the winter. They found a barren, nearly frozen land. In the middle of

November 1610, crew member John Williams died of exposure to the cold. Others came down with **scurvy**, a disease caused by a poor diet. Their gums turned black and rotted. Spots appeared all over their bodies. They lost their strength. Soon, Hudson's crew would be reduced to eating moss and frogs. Abacuk Prickett wrote that he would rather have eaten rotten wood. "To speak of all our trouble would be too tedious," he noted.

Somehow, the ragged crew made it through the wretched winter. Even in the coldest weather, they were able to hunt partridges. In the spring, they ate geese and ducks. The sailors made a drink from tree sap that they said improved their

The eastern coast of Hudson Bay is rocky.

Treating Scurvy

During Henry Hudson's time, people did not know what caused scurvy. In 1753, doctors made the connection between scurvy and diet. That year, a doctor in the British Navy named James Lind wrote that eating citrus fruits, rich in vitamin C, would prevent scurvy. The British Navy began feeding sailors oranges, lemons, and limes. By doing so, the navy greatly reduced the number of scurvy cases.

scurvy. In May 1611, the ice on the bay began to break up. The coming of spring did not improve the crew's spirits. They still distrusted Hudson. When an American Indian appeared at the crew's shelter, Hudson asked his crew to give him some of their personal belongings to use in trading. Only two of them agreed. Eventually, Hudson's hard bargaining drove the American Indian away. With him went any chance of help for Hudson and his crew.

By June 1611, the crew of the *Discovery* was ready to leave the scene of their miserable winter. Their troubles were by no means behind them, though. Their bread ran out very quickly. When a supply of cheese was handed out, the crew complained about the portions they were given.

Then Hudson made a fatal mistake. He ordered that the crew's sea chests be broken open and searched for bread. He believed that some crew members were hoarding supplies of bread. The sailors, however, considered their sea chests off-limits—even to the captain. To them, this was the worst thing Hudson had done. The captain found thirty loaves of bread hidden away. Angry with his crew, Hudson took the thirty loaves himself.

Set Adrift

The next night, members of the crew began planning their mutiny. On June 22, 1611, they acted. In the still of night, several of them seized Hudson. They tied Hudson's arms behind his back and put him into a small boat with his son and seven other sick sailors. The prisoners were allowed to take a few

This illustration shows Hudson's crew pushing him and his son toward a small boat that they would set adrift.

possessions with them in the boat. Then the mutineers cut the small boat free, and the *Discovery* sailed away.

Hudson, his son, and the rest of the sailors in the small boat tried to follow the ship. When the mutineers saw the small boat still following them, they "flew away as though from an enemy." Hudson and his small band of sailors were utterly alone. They were never seen again.

Twenty-one years later, an English sea captain discovered the remains of a cabin near Hudson Bay. Some historians think Hudson and his remaining crew may have built the cabin as they struggled to survive after the mutiny. But the remains of Henry Hudson and the others in the small boat were never found. As for the mutineers on board the *Discovery*, they had to endure a horrible journey home. Along the way, they were attacked by Inuit, natives of the Arctic coast. Five Englishmen died in the attack—including the leaders of the mutiny. In the middle of the ocean, the survivors ran out of food and had to eat bird bones and candle wax. They finally made their way back to England "more dead than alive." They had been gone more than sixteen months. Seven years after the mutiny, they were tried and found not guilty.

Hudson never found a water route to Asia. He lost his life looking for the Northwest Passage. Still, Hudson's achievements are remarkable. No other explorer mapped as much of the icy Arctic waters as Hudson. Other explorers gained glory in the warm southern seas, but Hudson never gave up pushing through fog, snow, ice, and bitter cold. His efforts laid the

Northwest Passage

The Northwest Passage is the name for the long-sought water route across North America. This route is a series of channels through the Arctic islands of Canada. Explorers searched for this route for centuries. In 1906, Norwegian explorer Roald Amundsen (center) was the first explorer to sail the Northwest Passage.

foundation for future exploration. His third voyage led to the Dutch colonization of the Hudson River valley. His final voyage laid the basis for English claims in Canada. All his explorations added to the growing knowledge of the world beyond Europe in the 1600s.

Timeline

c. 1570	Henry Hudson born.
April 23, 1607	Hudson leaves London as captain of the *Hopewell* on his first voyage of discovery.
April 22, 1608	Hudson leaves on second voyage on board the *Hopewell*.
April 6, 1609	*Half Moon* sets sail.
July 18, 1609	Hudson goes ashore in what is now Maine.
September 3, 1609	Hudson sails up what will become known as the Hudson River.
November 7, 1609	*Half Moon* returns to Dartmouth, England.
April 17, 1610	*Discovery* departs for North America.
August 2, 1610	Hudson comes to what is now Hudson Bay.
November 1610–May 1611	Hudson and crew winter on the southern shore of Hudson Bay.
June 22, 1611	Members of Hudson's crew mutiny and abandon him at sea.

Glossary

bark—a small sailing boat with three masts

cardamom—a plant native to Asia that has a small fruit whose seeds are used as a spice and in medicine

cask—a container shaped like a barrel that is used for holding liquid

charter—an official document granting, guaranteeing, or showing the limits of the rights and duties of the group to which it is given

cinnamon—a spice made from the inner bark of a tree native to eastern Asia

clove—the dried flower bud of a tropical tree used as a spice

floe—a flat mass of ice formed on the surface of a body of water

About the Author

Andrew Santella writes for publications such as *GQ* and the *New York Times Book Review*. He is the author of several books for young people: *Lewis and Clark*, *The War of 1812*, *Impeachment*, *Thomas Jefferson: Voice of Liberty*, *The Assassination of Robert F. Kennedy*, *The Chisholm Trail*, *The Capitol*, and *Mount Rushmore*. He is a graduate of Loyola University, and he lives in Chicago.